MOURNING FOR MY FATHER

Seymour Freedman

ISBN 965-229-048-3

Field Publishing House Ltd.
POB 6056, Jerusalem 91060 Israel.

Field Books/U.S.A
POB 101, Woodmere, N.Y. 11598

Printed in Israel

A word of dedication and apology

These lines are dedicated to those who knew my father best and loved him most deeply. They are not meant to be the story of his life, or a memorial portrait of him but rather the record of my own experience of grief after the passing of my father from this world. These lines emphasize certain sides of my father's character, at the expense of others which might seem more important to those who also knew and loved him. I pray to G-d that what I have omitted here, and what I have spoken of, will not cause any additional grief and suffering to those who have mourned for him as I have.

AFTER SHIVAH

After Shivah

After the most painful grief
come the longer days
of slower sadness.

I wait alone
deep in myself
with images of you
cutting my mind
from time to time
for greater pain.

The days ahead
in which I will never be
with you again
weigh on me.
And I fear
all my life will be
one long mourning
one sadness, unending always.

I did what I could do

I did what I could do
It wasn't much.

My father died,
I am crying still,
I will always cry.

Until they put me too
into the ground
in a box
it will never be warm in.

It is so painful to ask

Was the last struggle
the struggle for life,
or the struggle to be free
of your pain?

And was the silence and the quiet
which came after
a realization or an absence of feeling?

And did it end
as it should have ended,
as G-d demanded it end,
or could it have been kinder?

And shouldn't I
have stayed with you
when the nurse asked
that we leave?

Shouldn't I have been with you
at your last minute
in this world?
holding you in my arms
as you held your mother in yours
when she gave out
her last breath?
nearly thirty five long years,
one generation ago?

How can it be?

*How can it be
that my father died?
and will not be here again?*

*How can it be
that one who has been with me
all my life,
is suddenly not?*

*How can such unfairness be?
How can G-d have let this happen?*

Despite all my imaginings

Despite all my imaginings,
of life
in other worlds,

I cannot reconcile myself
to your not being here.

Despite all my imaginings of life on other worlds,
I act as if
this deathfilled earth
is G-d's only true world.

Let time and strangers

Let time and strangers
care for my father's memory.

I will care only for him,
who cannot have died.

The day you died the world persisted

The day you died
The world did not stop
even in your own small town
most went on with their lives
as if nothing
had happened.

The day you died
The world mocked
and cats and birds and ants
persisted.

The day you died
the world proved
it did not need you
for its existence.

And how I hated and resented
such a world,
how I wanted it
to die too.

And how it cared for me
as much as it cared for you.

You wanted so much

You wanted so much
in the last year
of your life
to come to the land of Israel.

And I delayed you.

Now if we meet here
it will be
after the dry bones
have risen
in another world.
After G-d, and you, if not myself,
have forgiven me.

Why does the human being

Why does the human being,
why did my father,
have to end his days
in suffering and pain?

Could not G-d who loves us,
find a more dignified and joyful way,
to deliver us?

Why didn't my father die peacefully
quietly
in his sleep,
without the restless struggling,
and the agony of the end?

Why did my father's last moments
have to be among
and like,
the most terrible
he had known
in his life?

The regret

We all failed you,
each in his own way.

We did not save you,

and those who love you most,
must live with regret
to the end of our days.

We who loved you most
did not save you.

And if the ground is the end

And if the ground is the end
and there is no more,
than dust to dust,
and we have said good-bye forever,
then I must wonder
why G-d
bothered creating creatures
in G-d's image,
why One who is Good
should deny life
to life's most remarkable creation.

If the ground is the end,
and there is no more,
than dust to dust,
then I must wonder
why G-d
created us at all,
and how the children of our Father
could be abandoned by Him,
so cruelly.

I dare not go deep in memory

I dare not go deep in memory,
yet the pain comes.
I need to talk with you,
I see you in my mind
and know
I will never hear you again
in this world.
I dare not go deep in memory,
and yet the pain comes.

Only my brother and sister

Only my brother and sister
wept as I wept:
only they too
lost a father.

So I must not bring

So I must not bring
my pain and disorder
to the others,
who have enough
of their own.

I must instead
bring quiet strength:
calm
and an understanding
which lessens
their loneliness.

I must be strong
insofar as I can,
for those who survived,
for those you would have me
care for.

It is a dream

It is a dream,
and I am going to awake,
and you are going to be here
as you always were:
Nothing has changed,
nothing is going to change.
You are my father,
and I am your child,
and we go on living
forever and ever
without interruption,
as we did in the past
before this terrible dream,
this nightmare, this illusion
happened.

I feared its happening

I feared its happening
year after year,
and when it did not,
believed it would not.

Then the phone call came,
and the struggle
in the hospital,
and the grave,
and the shiva.

And I somehow still
do not believe
it happened,

or that I
was so,
am so,
terribly surprised.

There had been so many other tearful departures

There had been so many other tearful departures
which I thought might be the last
and were not.

Oh why couldn't there have been just one more time
and one more time,
and one more time?

Why did there have to be
a final goodbye?

After years of guilt and blame

After years of guilt and blame
came the happy years,
when I knew my father's love
and acceptance.

Why did life have to end,
just when it had become so good?
why after all the long years of suffering,
couldn't the few years of happiness
have been longer?

They say 'Time heals'

They same "Time heals"
and "He had a good life"
and "He was over eighty, an old man after all"
and "Lucky that he did not suffer so much"

And I do not reply
and the grief wells up inside,
and the pain tears through me
And I do not reply.

In your fear for us, your children

In your fear for us, your children,
you loved us,
when we did not know:
In your fear
for yourself
You moved us to love you more
in trying to help you.

In the end
for us,
there was no fear of you
but love, only love.

And this love
we will bear with us always.

SHELOSHIM TO YAHRTZEIT

Sheloshim

My father, my father
thirty nights
(under the ground)
away from us.

And it is just beginning.
It is just beginning.

I never imagined

I never imagined
my father dying,

I never imagined,
it would happen
as it happened

I, the expert of anticipations,
never came close to imagining
what reality
turned to be.

And in this too
I now more deeply know
my limitations.
Death humiliating
in more ways
than one.

Because no words can say

Because no words can say
what you are to us,

No words can tell
what your presence is.

And I have words, only words,
words of my own,
words of others,
to console me,

when I do not wish to be consoled,
but want you
to be here
with us,
as you always have been.

And if I die

And if I die,
and continue to die?
and if death become all I am?
Dying Dying Dying
day after day?

And if I die,
and continue to die?

Will these years
of self-pity
cry then for me
as they cry now for you,
my Father,
who died,
without dying,

AND WHO WILL NEVER DIE?

Why does G-d create...

Why does G-d create
such a remarkable being
only to let him be
as an ant,
in an instant
crushed to dust?

Why does G-d's greatest creation
have such a small life,
when dumb worlds
and cosmoses of distance
stretch on and on
without interruption?

Why does what we most love,
the creature created in G-d's image,
die?
when what is evil and indifferent
recurs and recurs and recurs?
Why?

When not thinking to,
I also remember you

When not thinking to, I also remember you,
by frowning as you would frown,
by smiling as you would smile,
in a word or phrase which comes to mind,
as you would have said it.
A sudden image, a picture of your face,
in my mind,
a soul-cry at your absence.
When not thinking to, I also remember you.

So what does death bring..

So what does death bring,
but more death?
sin inviting sin?
Pain, pain,
disorder, disorder,
loss and madness?

Oh that I were far far away
from myself
in some distant realm
of darkness,
where even fear
had a new name,
and was not called 'my father's death.'

Better to not have suffered

Better to not have suffered
long and slow deterioration
Better not to have ended
in humiliation.
Better not to have been left alone
unable to care for yourself.
Better that the last night
of your life
you could speak and smile
with your sons and granddaughter.
Better this way,
than so many others.
And yet

Would it have never been
at all.

These regrets will always be with me

The nurse who controlled the sips of liquid
you so thirsted for.

The doctor who tested your mind
with a subtraction problem
you once
would have laughed at.

All of us
who could not answer
the agony and fear
in your eyes
in your last moments
of struggle.

All these humiliations
I will always regret
not sparing you from.

All the pains
I so much wanted to
save you from

and did not.

I hope this consolation, Dad

Four months,
not long:
You see me,
hear me,
pray for you
each day.
I hope this consolation, Dad.
You know now more than ever,
how much your children love you.
I hope this consolation, Dad.
Dad?

I cannot ask G-d

I cannot ask G-d
to bring you back
to earth.

I do ask G-d
to enable us
to live together
in a higher world,

even though I know
G-d has not promised us this.

There was so much

There was so much
I didn't know how to
ask you
to remember.

And now
It is gone with you
to another world, forever.

Death has saddened memory

Death has saddened memory,
and the consolation I once knew
of making past life live for present
can be no longer.

To remember you now
is to know
you will never be here
with me again.

Death has saddened memory,
and in pain
frightened it away.

Where?

If there is no life
under the ground
then the peace
of the cemetery
is not felt by him
either.

And we must look
for his perception
and feeling
in some other place
we in this world
do not and cannot ever know.

But where? and when? and how?

When you lived I did not mourn

When you lived
I did not mourn
your youth lost
or all the stages in aging
to old age.

But now
it is not only you,
as you were in the last years,
but all the selves you were
which I am lonely for,
and for my own past times
as I was with you
through them.

Why there should be Death I understand

Why there should be Death I understand,
why you had to die I cannot understand.

G-d does not reply
to each of my demands
as if I were
the ruler of the world.
A Father
sometimes understands
why saying 'no' now
is necessary
for a greater good later.

I hold myself back

I hold myself back,
I do not let myself
have certain thoughts,
I protect myself
against the pain.

The famous 'would have been, could have been, should have been'
you so long tormented yourself with
are stricken from my mind.

From your great suffering
I have studied how to
suffer as little as possible.

And in this too, my one true teacher,
your example has been my guide and my help.

Even when you did not know you were doing it,
you protected me my father,
from our worst self.

I did not make your name in greatness

I did not make your name in greatness
I thought
we would wait together forever
until you saw
your own justification
in the greatness
of your son.

But not in this world, Dad.
I did not do for you
what I dreamed,
I did not give you
what I believed
you needed to have.
A name and a greatness
beyond the one you could make
for yourself.

I did not justify you, Dad,
and perhaps it was not my place to.

But I will regret not doing it, always.

All my thought of Death beforehand

All my thought of Death beforehand,
all my understanding,
did not teach me,
what Death is.

Only through your death,
have I come to know Death,
and in truth,
I have learned, now,
all I ever want
to know,
though not, I fear,
all I will come to know.

It was an old man

It was an old man,
who could barely shuffle along,
a bent backed old man,
who died.

And yet there also died with him
the tall and strong young father
pulling on the sleigh
through the winter snows
of childhood.
The Children,
who will never be children again.

I am crying for myself Dad

I am crying for myself Dad
not for you
the way you cried
for yourself
all those years.
selfishly,
with an inability to understand
anything
but your own pain.

Now I can be the selfish one, Dad,
though I don't want to,
though I hate it.
Now I can cry night and day
for myself
without thinking of others.

Forgive me, Dad,
Forgive me Ma and Jakie and Joycie,
Forgive me G-d.

I know how you suffer too
and I do love you
and I feel your pain also,
though I cry and cry
for the father
I have lost.

I do not think

I do not think
because it does not help
to think.

Only at Kaddish each day
does the pain return
with your image.

I do not think
because it does not help
to think.

The higher mercy

I know your errors and even your sins,
I know G-d had the right to punish you.
But you are my father
and G-d is the G-d of mercy
and I prayed you would always be forgiven
never punished with death.

And now I pray
G-d having punished you once
taken you from this world
continues to forgive you
in the higher world
where for the great and the good as you
there is only mercy and more mercy.

My grief is from G-d

My grief is from G-d,
as is my fear
that G-d will deny
your being immortal.

My trust in G-d
is from G-d,
as is my distrust.

G-d must not care for me to be silent,
otherwise I would not be writing this.

G-d must demand I remember you, my father,
otherwise
my writing this,
all I do,
is in vain.

How can I reconcile my belief

How can I reconcile my belief
that life is a unique story,
which can be told only once,
with my desire to have you with me,
forever?

How can I reconcile my belief,
in the necessity of death,
with my inability
to leave you?

How can I reconcile
what I believe,
with what I hope,
what I know,
with what I love?

How can I reconcile
what cannot be reconciled,
how can I console myself,
when I cannot be consoled?

How empty I am of words of comfort and exaltation

How empty I am
of words of comfort
and exaltation.
How plain my heart is,
how bereft of inspiration.

I cannot now sing praises to G-d,
Psalms are beyond these lines,
in feeling also
and in tone.

Simple lines
of my own thought
and feeling
are my writing now.

Words of grief
and love for you,
which in their style too
feel empty and deprived.

I don't ask

I don't ask
for the colossus
of my youth
the giant
of my childhood.

Only for that old,
whitehaired,
bentbacked man
who less than a year ago,
shuffled happily up the hill
to the house.

I don't ask
for him
in power and strength.

But only as he was,
when I last saw him.

Dad, why did you have to go?
Why did you have to die?

I so miss you.
It is so lonely
without you.

Why my father must live

I do not claim
you should live
because you were the most righteous
or most just

I do not say G-d could not find
Sin and Blemish in you,
I do not find after you death
a false perfection in you.

But only that I love you, my father,
beyond justice and perfection
and righteousness and goodness
just as you were and are,
and will always be for me,
my father, my one my only, father.

'Why can't you just one more time?'

Why can't you
just one more time
come into the room
where your wife is waiting
and tell your family
the story
of the day's adventure?

Who would it hurt
after all
if you still lived?
Who would it do
any harm to?

I bear the rage of my own grief

I bear the rage of my own grief,
without knowing who to blame,
For who says the son can have more love
for his father,
than G-d for His children?
For who says the son dare complain
for a father taken from him in heroic old age?
For where is the human being,
however great or good,
who will not die?
I bear the rage of my own grief,
without knowing who to blame.
I bear the rage of my own grief.

Does G-d need my prayer

Can G-d need my prayer
to inspire help for my father?

Can G-d need my prayer
to increase G-d's love
for my father?

Does G-d need my prayer
to enable me to believe myself
helping my father?

Does G-d need my prayer
to help me?

And would G-d help my father and me,
whether I pray or not?

And does G-d help us more,
because I pray?

And is my prayer for G-d
proof of my love of my father,
proof of my love of G-d?

Does my prayer really help
my father and me?
Does it help G-d?

Does G-d enable us to help G-d,
in our prayer?

Does G-d need my prayer,
because G-d loves me and my father?

At suppertime

At suppertime now
Ma is alone.

You made it all so difficult Dad,
And all so interesting.

It is so quiet now: too quiet.

Poor Ma, poor, poor Ma.

If I were wise and understanding

If I were wise and understanding
I would thank G-d
for your long life,
for you not having died earlier,
when your leaving the world
might not have been secretly greeted
even by those who love you
as relief from suffering.

If I were wise and understanding
I would thank G-d
for having taken you, now,
when you so much loved life,
and when we so much wanted you to live,
for taking you,
against our will.

If I were wise and understanding
I would thank G-d,
for enabling us
to accuse G-d and G-d alone
for having taken you,
for having freed us
of the guilt
which would have come
had you died
in an earlier time of your life,
a time when your suffering
made us hate life, also.

If I were wise and understanding
I would thank G-d,
for having taken you
after a long and full life
in a time you knew life as good.

If I were wise and understanding
I would thank G-d
for leaving us all in longing
and prayer,
all in deep need
for the continuation
of your life,
in G-d's other world.

I do not know if it is consolation for you

I do not know
if it is consolation to you now,
But you did not live your life
for nothing.
You made something of it.
You left behind a family
who loves you,
the children and grandchildren,
and their love for you
which will go on and on,
until we ourselves
are too, if worthy,
granted our own consolation.

In the days of your most terrible pain

In the days of your most terrible pain,
when you could not scream Time to an end,
You did not know, you did not see, you could not feel,
how brief this life would be,
how quickly it would end.

In the days of your most terrible pain.

Once I needed to justify your suffering

Once I needed to justify your suffering
through proving your greatness to the world,

Now it is you I miss,
not what you might become,

My heart is not
in making of my father
a great man
mankind will worship,
but in being with you
here and now.

A New Year will begin soon

A New Year will begin soon
the first without my father:
Last year I did not pray
in fear enough,
took repentance for granted.

And this year
it is already too late.
Yet never too late.

So in greater fear
for those remaining
in this world,
and those already
in the other,
I will pray and pray and pray

for G-d's mercy,
upon all those
I love.

I did not speak with you of death

I did not speak with you of death,
I did not want even to raise the possibility
that you would not get better.

Now I wonder
if you wanted to share your fears,
and were not comforted
by such considerate silence.

I do not know,
I will never know,
if I lessened your suffering,
or increased it.

And if this loss of only one

And if this loss
of only one,
and in his old age,
and after a full life,
and if this loss
of only one
should bring
such unbearable
grief,

then how do those
bear their grief
who have suffered
more violently
and more unjustly
the loss
of their children,
their whole family?

How do human beings bear so much
when I find it impossible to bear
even one somewhat understandable loss?

Or is sanity a broader concept than I can understand
and madness too more real than it seems?

No more having to do what you hated

No more having to do
what you hated,
no more decisions
you could not make,
no more rage contained,
humiliations suffered silently,
in the making of a living
for your family.

No more disturbances, troubles, problems,
but what you cried for again and again
in your life
and found only in your last years,
peace of mind,
a calm happiness
with which G-d blesses
the redeemed,
forever.

After all the years

After all the years
even the most difficult times
are remembered
with a kind of longing and love.

I see you in the junk shop
on one of those interminable Saturdays
making order, which is more disorder,
out of the hundreds of drums and bails
and pieces of 'usable'
scattered everywhere.
I grow frightened
as you shout
and with each outburst of anger
become more angry.
I watch as in impatience,
you make us 'step aside'
and begin loading by yourself
the low-foss on the truck.

Pictures, innumerable pictures
of you at different places
and at different times,
torment my mind.

And they are my childhood and my life,
with you.

And I long for them and miss them,
as I long for you my father
all what has passed for you
having passed for me also,
and your life, my life also,
never to return again.

Why?

I don't look for you,
I don't expect to see you,
I don't wait to hear your voice.

But sometimes
when I am somewhere else
suddenly
I feel your absence
and begin to cry.

Why can't you listen
to this music
with me now?
Why can't you feel
the joy and beauty
of life,
even in all its sadness?

Why can't you feel the wind,
and see the blue sky in the distance,
the flowing Hudson
you always loved?
and ride along singing in the truck
on one of your good days
to make another payload?

Why is so much you once loved
denied you?
and your presence denied me?

Why is their Death,
and Why is their Absence,
and Why is their Loneliness
in this world?

A father gave his children dreams

A father gave his children dreams,
and each took some small part
as his legacy.
And concentrated
in his own way
to realize for you
some dream
you could not for yourself.
Your oldest son in business,
your second son in Israel,
your daughter in teaching,
in work which is clean.

Each of your children,
made of your dream
their opportunity
and will work for you
as for themselves
to the end
of our lives.

Without your kind of humor

How much poorer
life is for me now
without your kind of humor,
without my being able to enjoy
a story of yours.

Dad, if we could only talk together,
the way we did
these last years
how happy I would be,
how grateful I would feel.

But it is not to be,
not in this world,anyway.

You longed for greatness in the world

You longed for greatness in the world
and never understood
the greatness of your own mind.
You dreamed
and hated yourself
for being only a dreamer.
You did not understand
your true greatness
in that complicated world
of feeling.
You suffered inside.

Dreamer of dreams,
master of contradictions
who feared and hoped
into meaning
higher worlds
from minor possibilities,
who left your children
an inheritance in humiliations
we must give our lives to redeem.
Great inspirer and teacher
of the minds, hidden wonders
and pains,
the greatest father
another lonely
dreamer of dreams
could ever hope
to have been blessed with.

There is no pain, Dad

There is no pain, Dad,
no pain.
The snakepit never got you,
no one demands of you now
anything you cannot do.
The pressure is off,
you don't have to be a merchant prince or sports hero,
or anything you yourself are not sure
you want to be.
Your brothers are not your responsibility.
You don't have to get up in the winter dark
and in the freezing cold morning start up the old truck.
You don't have to deal with the jakey bums.
You don't have to flatter and soft talk.
No one asks you to make a good living anymore.
You don't have to service your accounts.
You don't have to be polite to people
you have contempt for.
No one demands anything of you anymore, Dad,
No humiliations, no doing what you hated to do
against your will and conscience,
The pressure is off,
It's easy now, Dad,
You can rest,
rest forever,
the way you did
in the last few
good years
of your life.
You can rest,
and I pray,
enjoy yourself,
for you certainly
earned this.

In the dirt in the ground

In the dirt
in the ground
subject to the worms
in humiliation
dust to dust.

Tell me, you do not lie there,

Tell me the grave
is only a marker
that we survivors need
to return to
because we cannot yet know
the true place..

Tell me you are not there..

Please G-d, tell me my father, heart and soul and mind,
is with You,
and tall and strong
as in the days of his youth
preparing for the time
when his family
will be with him
again.

Tell me you wait there for us,
and our dying too
is only
a coming home to you, closer to G-d.

The righteous Jew

Joe Bedell and Rossoff
and Freeman Neilson,
Just a few of the lonely characters,
you time and again visited
and were kind to.

The goodness and compassion and charity
will I pray
stand as evidence
in time of judgment,
that you in your best days
loved justice, did mercy
walked humbly with your G-d,
as the righteous Jew
is commanded to do
generation to generation.

Of that dark family

You were the last of the sons to leave the world,
of that dark family,
which suffered more than it lived.

You were the chosen one
of your mother,
the protector of the rest,
the single success
of those lost from the beginning.

You were the
deepest and most despairing
champion of the Freedman sufferers,
great hero of the most terrible depths,
Lonely, lonely prisoner in yourself,

Who in the last years,
thanks to G-d's grace
and your wife and daughter's care,
escaped the curse,
remade your life
in a happiness and contentment
your own parents had never known.

Have I forgotten...

Have I forgotten
the yelling and the accusations,
the times of anger,
when you blamed one of us
for something we had not done?

Have I forgotten
the abuse
for no reason,
the humiliation
which brought such torment
in our powerlessness to help you,
or ourselves?

Have I forgotten
the anger and the hatred,
the fear
you instilled in us
with all your suffering?

Have I forgotten
you at your worst,
all those years
when Ma taught us,
never to blame you
but always to love and respect you
no matter what?
All those years
when it was Ma
who was the family
and saved you for us?

My memory of you too

My memory of you too
is already a recreation
of many different rememberings.

And yet there are specific moments
which return with such clearness
and intensity,
that death seems to be only
the inability
to live those moments again
as if
for the first time.

We are on the roof of the place in seventh avenue
in the dead of winter
and you bring the steaming coffee
to the frozen snow-shovelers:
You are angry and impatient,
swinging the big sledge hammer
breaking cast-iron in the yard:
You are crying in the backbedroom
and will not get up for breakfast.
You are pulling us on the sleigh
through the silent Sunday distances,
You are the smiling gentleman
saying 'how do' to the ladies,
greeted by your 'friends'
in each office you hate going to.
You are saying Kiddush on Friday night
after we have waited for you
to come home late from work.

You are and you are and you are,
and there is no end to my memories of you
which I against my will
turn to again
since they are the only presence of you
I now have.

The way you...

The humor and the heat,
your way of playing
and your way of fighting,
and above all,
your way of working,
your kindness, when you had the mood,
and your charity for life's underdogs,
your hatred of the false and phony would-be bigshots,
the way you did not know and understand so many things,
and the way you in a deeper way
felt more than all of us.
The way you were so many things,
and dreams,
so many dimensions of experience,
so many complications and complexities,
the way you were many human beings
in one.
The way you were always struggling with yourself,
your own worst enemy,
the way you were so much,
so much more,
than any human being I have known
has been.
The way you laughed and the way you cried,
and the way you froze out in silence,
or ziddled out in anger,
the way you smiled,
and the way you laughed,
the way you worked harder than ten men one week,
and stopped working the next,
the way you suffered,

the way you reluctantly enjoyed,
the way you loved without knowing how to say you loved,
the way you provided so well, and could not help in anything at all.
The way were so much more
than any human being I have known
has been.

Without great suffering

Without great suffering,
and after the happiest years
of his life,
and surrounded by loving family.

It is possible to imagine a far worse Death.

And perhaps this explains,
why I am not angry at G-d:
and do not curse His mercy,

If I am nonetheless
not happy with it either.

There's a smile you have Dad

There's a smile you have, Dad,
which no one else has,
or will ever have.

I want to see that smile again.
I want to see you again,
Dad.

Want and want and want —

In grief as in love

In grief as in love
there is the inner circle
of the very few,
and the nothing of all the rest.

All the words
of friends,
all the kindness and consideration
of strangers
are a distant murmuring only.

We live for a few,
and die for a few,
and our only true heartfelt cries
only for the few
who we love.

My father's last word

My father's last word
was a scream:
He died as he often lived,
fighting the pain.

May G-d grant him
what his restless soul
most longed for.
Not an easy peace,
but the peace won
through a lifetime
of hard work,
as victory,
as vengeance.

All your life you complained

All your life
you complained.
But when the real sickness came
you said nothing
and went to the end,
as if you did not wish
to cause those who loved you
any more suffering.

After such a long hard road
so kind
in the end.

The dream of greatness must not die

Greater than any other great man
will ever be for me.

You, the colossus of my childhood,
the form of greatness itself
have gone to another world.

And there is no greatness anymore
But only middle-aged life
with all its minor problems.

And yet somehow I know
because you are in me,
the dream of greatness
will return,
and we will at last
stride through the world
as we have dreamed,
achieving a greatness
even our worst enemies
will wonder at.

I disappointed you my father

I was not the athlete you wanted me to be,
nor am I the teacher either:

I disappointed you my father,
and this I tell myself
was done so that I might in some way
deeper than you could imagine
realize your greatest dreams for you.

But you did not see this on earth,
and it was my dream that you would.

I have not only disappointed you, my father...

I was not a bad son

I was not a bad son
and my heart was in helping you
I was not a bad son
not willfully disobedient or evil
I was not a bad son
But could have been better.

What did I do for my father?

What did I do for my father?

I lived in Israel
as he had always dreamed to,
and this made him proud.

I gave him the pleasure
of two more grandchildren.

I was educated formally
as he would have been.

I loved him,
and he knew this.

Each thing I do as if I were you

Each thing I do,
as if I were you.

I will swim again in the sea,
remembering how you loved to.

I will swim again for you.
And the stroke I take
will be the stroke you taught me.

Only when I look to the side,
you will not be there.

Each thing I do,
as if I were you.

Nonetheless

Nonetheless with loving children
and grandchildren
gathered around you—
nonetheless in a heroic old age,
nonetheless without terrible prolonged suffering
at the end:
nonetheless, if it had to end,
and it always has to end,
it ended for you
better than for most.
Nonetheless.

Saying Kaddish

*Saying Kaddish
is the one act
of love and help
I do for you
each day.*

I fear my protest will anger G-d

I fear my protest will anger G-d.
I know it is a sin to grieve too much.
After all four score years in strength
is a life of blessing.

To ask for life
to go on without end
is to demand
what cannot be given.

I should compel myself to greater inner quiet,
to silence and acceptance:
I should not feel it right
that I grieve so...

I should somehow be and feel
what all my heart and soul
are not...

I should... and I cannot...

How I would be happy, Dad

How I would be happy
if I could know for certain
that there is G-d's other world,

And you are there,
happy in mind,
carefree of the earth,
observing your children
with a sense that all will be alright
for them one day too
in G-d's higher world.

How I would be happy, Dad,
to know you are happy there
and that when my time comes
we will be together again
looking down with calm
on the generations
upon generations
of our descendants
to come.

How I would be happy now here, Dad,
to know that you are happy there
in G-d's other, higher world.

I am growing cold

I am growing cold, Dad,
moving farther and farther away,
losing my will
to speak
with you

The pain of understanding,
that my cries
do not cause you
to answer,
deters me.

I must protect myself,
in distance,
and be cold,
and pretend
I don't need to hear.

I am going away
for a while Dad,
until the time comes
when I can return
without its hurting so much.

Wasn't it right?

Wasn't it right
that you who struggled so
in your life,
should not go out quietly
but in an agony
of resistance?

Wasn't it right
that you came to death
at the moment
that death seemed better
than a life of such suffering
and incapacity?

Wasn't it right
that you died
when you did
in heroic old age,
that you died
how you did
in fierce struggle,
that you died,
in character
and in keeping
with the way
you lived?

You died, and all the years

You died,
And all the years
which had gone by unnoticed
became suddenly,
more than half my life lost.

You died,
and I became
a middle-aged man
growing older too fast.

You died,
and reminded me
that if I do not wake up
it soon will be over
before I know it
without my having done
what I promised myself
so long ago
I would do for your name.

If I had been more experienced in death

If I had been more experienced in death,
I would have seen the signs,
and not deluded myself about recovery,
I would have stayed with you to the very end,
and not listened to the nurses:
I would have said the right prayer,
I would have chosen the pallbearers,
and known every word of the kaddish at the grave.

If I had been more experienced,
I would not have made those mistakes,
which did not make any great difference
in the world,
and hopefully
are forgiven by G-d,
and will not do you harm
where you are now.

I will get on the plane

I will get on the plane
to go home again
and it will be
the first time
You will not be there
to meet me.

Where is my home, now, Dad?
Where are you?

When the time comes to stop saying Kaddish

When the time comes to stop saying Kaddish,
what will I say?

How will I in serving G-d help you, my father?
How will I in some way continue to think that somehow
I might be helping you, my father?

And what will I do with all this grief,
which still has not gone away?

By the depth of our mourning

By the depth of our mourning
we show the strength
of our love
for you.

And yet all our grief,
all our weeping and sorrow,
seem to me at times
nothing other than
the expression of the helplessness
of that love.

But then I ask,
must not G-d too most specially love one
whose family loves him so much?
Must not G-d too see in our love
still more reason
to continue loving,
loving and caring
for you,
now that we cannot?

In Kaddish

In Kaddish
To exalt the name of G-d
for your sake,
to praise G-d
so that you will be better judged.

And in praising, pray
that your Creator
and the Creator of all I love
will save you,
will answer us
in the world which goes on forever,
the world in which nothing need ever die again.

The end of saying Kaddish

Everything must come to an end:
and though we don't believe
it will happen.
It does happen.

Next week
I will finish eleven months
of saying Kaddish.

Leaves will fall
from other trees,
The sky will hear the cries
of other voices.

G-d knows
and will know
that though
I no longer say Kaddish aloud
Kaddish is in me now,
and will be repeated
time after time
for the rest
of my life.

There is no Kaddish

There is no Kaddish
to say anymore.
Still the days pass.

I don't know
where I am in the world:

A child
without a father.
Forty-six years old.

And now after all the talk

And now, after all the talk
and weeping
over him
comes a need for silence.

It is too painful
for me
to speak about my father
with anyone
except with those
who knew and loved him.

And with myself,
with whom I do not stop speaking
of him.

This oppressive grief and this all pervading sadness

This oppressive grief,
and this all pervading Sadness,

which have become my life,
after the time
of acutest grief
supposedly gone.

This oppressive grief,
and this all pervading sadness
which seems to have become
reason for itself
dominating my life,
without any thought of you,
its cause and its feeling.

This oppressive grief,
and this all pervading Sadness
which is more sad,
when it is senseless and selfish,
no help for you.

This oppressive grief
and this all pervading Sadness.

I walked alone tonight

I walked alone tonight,
The way you loved to walk
far and into the distance.

I walked alone tonight,
and you were young,
and I was the child with you,
and the night was deep,
and the stars were near,
and the future was ours,
father and son.

I walked alone tonight.

One year has gone by

One year has gone by,
since you left this world.

You are with me,
and will be,
so long as I live.

One year has gone by
since you left this world.

You are with me,
and will be,
so long as I live.

AFTER ONE YEAR

Once I thought

Once I thought
of all my private evils
as temporary unpleasantness
I would in time overcome.

But now
your absence
will be with me
to the end
of my life.

And I will live always
in a world
which can never
be made
completely alright.

And when all your enemies are dead

And when all your enemies are dead,
and no one remembers
those who humiliated you,
and when so many who seemed to shine
in your time above you
have been forgotten,
Mankind will remember you,
will know and wonder at
the greatness of your struggle in mind,
will celebrate the language of your imagination,
the contradictions of your character.

For all the humiliations you knew
in your lifetime, my father,
there will be revenge in posterity,
and the name and reputation
you so cared for
will be in fame
in generations to come,
above and beyond
what you longed for it to be
in the days on earth,
when you were still dreaming.

Is there somewhere, anywhere...

Is there somewhere, anywhere,
in any world,
my father's awareness
of my thoughts now?

Is there somewhere, anywhere
in any world,
my father's feeling
of how deeply we love him
how greatly we miss him,
how now too,
life is so much sadder
for us
without him?

Is there somewhere, anywhere
in any world,
my father
who feels our love now?

Pirke Avot

Every man's father,
is his first best teacher:

My father taught more
than my lifetime has given me
to learn.

For the rest of my days
I will continue striving
to learn from my teacher.

Erev Shabbat I say Kiddush

Erev Shabbat I say Kiddush,
and hear you saying it.
My childhood returns
in the words of your blessing,
I see your smile, hear your voice,
Life is sacred again,
and Love is one generation teaching another
the creation of G-d.

It was not given

What is life,
that we love it so,
and do not wish
those we love
to ever leave it?

For you to simply walk outside,
to feel the fresh air,
to gaze in the distance.
To say a word here
or have a small conversation there.
To feel the joy of breathing
simply breathing
in the world.

How I prayed
you would leave the hospital
to see the world one more time,
only that.
But it was not given,
it was not given.

Because the simplest pleasure

Because the simplest pleasure
came with such difficulty for you,
You taught us all
the deepest appreciation
of each moment of joy in life.

Because you knew so much suffering,
you taught us
the slightest happiness,
a great gift.

Because you knew so much of life's pain,
you taught us to appreciate G-d's blessings,
because of you,
we learned to love in the deepest way
the goodness of G-d's world.

By loving my father

By loving my father,
and trying to help him
I pray more intensely each day.
I learn to love G-d more.

By loving my father,
I help myself,
I learn to love G-d more.

It was as if in these last years

It was as if in these last years
the conflict went out of our lives
and relationship.

And in some new and quiet acceptance
in love,
We moved through past and present
in happiness
and harmony,
deep as our common remembrance
of all the long years of our family life together,
father and son
at last
as father and son
should be.

Your death makes me see death differently also

Your death makes me see death differently also:
It is not simply
my loss of this earth
and this world.

It is the passageway
to meeting
with those I love
who have gone
before me.

It is the passageway
preceding
the final reunion
in which all those I love
will be
forever together
in the happiness
of our love.

Your death has made me lose my fear of my own death

Your death
has made me lose
my fear of my own death.
for if it happened to you,
then why shouldn't it happen to me?
and where you have gone
I must go also.

Still I pray to G-d
my life will not end
before my children
with children of their own,
before my work finished.

When my time comes,
then we must see each other again.

Was it your last agony..

Was it your last agony
which is your final judgment
of your life?
Or the torment of the middle years,
or the happiness of the final ones?

Which of your many judgments of yourself
stands as the true and ultimate one?

And why is it so important
for me to feel
that you somehow, in the end, ultimately
affirmed the goodness of your own life,
believed that it was all worthwhile,
not in vain?

My father's last years

Thank you G-d
for this blessing
of my father's last years

of a man happier in his old age
than at any other stage of his life.

Thank you G-d
for those last happy years
which somehow seemed
reward and compensation
for all the terrible years of suffering,
for all the punishment and pain.

Thank you G-d
for those last happy years
in which my father
no longer needed to conquer
the world
and was content to be
the 'king of Centerview Drive'.

Thank you G-d
for this blessing
that my father's last years
on earth
were happy ones.

Time does not make my sadness any less

Time does not make my sadness any less,
Time does not make my memory any less painful,
Time does not change
and Time will not change
what I have lost
and what I will always love.

There is no time,
There is only grief and mourning
for what happened once
and will last forever.

It happened now

It happened now
because G-d commanded it
to happen now.
And it is part of G-d's plan
which I cannot see.

As when I die,
it too will be part of G-d's plan
which others will not see
and I may then be revealed
the reason of.

It is a sin to grieve too much

It is a sin to grieve too much,
and we who loved him greatly, have greatly sinned,
and suffered even more greatly for this,
I nonetheless pray these words honor him,
written as they are in Love,
in accordance with G-d's commandment.

My grief for you

My grief for you
is also
my pity
for myself.

I cry
at what
I have
lost,

as well
as for the world
you no longer
see.

I cry too
for all those
you and I love
who loved you
as I do.

I weep for you, for myself, for all of us,
Pity for myself, pity for others,
Pain and sorrow
which does not end.

Since I 'lost' my father

Since I 'lost' my father,
whoever loses anyone
is a source of sorrow
for me.

I hear the grief of others
and it pains me back
to memory
of my own.

I sympathize with
every suffering being
because
I am one of them.

Grief is not my grief alone,
yet in our common humanity
there is no consolation,
but only pain
continual unending
ever new and renewed
pain and suffering.

I hear the grief of others,
and it only re-agonizes my own.

I will never believe

I will never believe
that your death is the last of your life,
and that your passing from this world
your loss forever.

I will never believe
that G-d
would let His beloved child
pass from this world,
never to live again.

I know you are alive somehow
in G-d's care,
in the heart and in the mind,
of the One who loves us all.

Time will not make me love you less

Time will not make me love you less,
but will I pray diminish the pain,
so that I can remember you,
and all the times of our life together,
not simply with sadness,
but with a sense of blessedness and gratitude.
No one in the world ever had
a father,
difficult in greatness, interesting in complexity,
as you, Dad.
I thank G-d for every moment we had together,
even the most painful ones,
I thank G-d for having given me you as a father,
I thank G-d, I thank you Dad,
I will love you always.